Measuring Time

Seasons of the Year

Tracey Steffora

Heinemann Library
Chicago, Illinois

www.heinemannraintree.com
Visit our website to find out
more information about
Heinemann-Raintree books.

To order:

☎ Phone 888-454-2279

💻 Visit www.heinemannraintree.com
to browse our catalog and order online.

Edited by Tracey Steffora and Dan Nunn
Designed by Richard Parker
Picture research by Hannah Taylor
Originated by Capstone Global Library Ltd
Printed and bound in the United States of America,
North Mankato, MN

14 13 12 11 10
10 9 8 7 6 5 4 3 2 1

Library of Congress Cataloging-in-Publication Data
Steffora, Tracey.
 Seasons of the year / Tracey Steffora.
    p. cm.—(Measuring time)
 Includes bibliographical references and index.
 ISBN 978-1-4329-4902-0 (hc)—ISBN 978-1-4329-4909-9 (pb) 1.
Seasons—Juvenile literature. 2. Time—Juvenile
literature. 3. Time measuremet—Juvenile literature. I. Title.
 QB637.4.S725 2011
 508.2—dc22
            2010028871

Acknowledgments
We would like to thank the following for permission to reproduce
photographs: Alamy Images pp. **4** (©Cultura), **15** (©RubberBall),
22 top right (©Jon Helgason); Corbis pp. **5** (epa/Kay Nietfeld),
21 (Blend Images/Jamie Grill/JGI); istockphoto pp. **6** (©Ermin
Gultenberger), **14** (©LeoGrand), **16** (©Primary Picture), **19**
(©Morley Read), **22 bot** (©mammamaart), **22 top left** (©David
Safanda); NASA p. **23 top**; Photolibrary pp. **10** (Comstock),
18 (Superstock); shutterstock pp. **7** (©Kai Schirmer), **8** (©Foto
Yakov), **11** (©Nagel Photography), **12** (©RazvanZinica), **13**
(©Shebeko), **17** (©Dennis Donohue), **20** (©Graeme Dawes), **23
bot** (oriontrail).

Front cover photographs of sunflowers reproduced with
permission of Alamy Images (©David Norton Photograghy),
autumn leaves reproduced with permission of Alamy Images
(©Bob Handelman), frosted pine needles reproduced with
permission of Alamy Images (©Christina Bollen) and tree bud
reproduced with permission of Photolibrary (Mixa). Back cover
photograph of a person sliding down a snowy hill reproduced
with permission of istockphoto (© Ermin Gultenberger).

Every effort has been made to contact copyright holders of
any material reproduced in this book. Any omissions will
be rectified in subsequent printings if notice is given to
the publisher.

Contents

Time and Seasons

Time is how long something takes.

Time is when things happen.

Some things take a short time.

Some things take a long time.

A season is a long amount of time.

spring

summer

fall

winter

There are four seasons in one year.

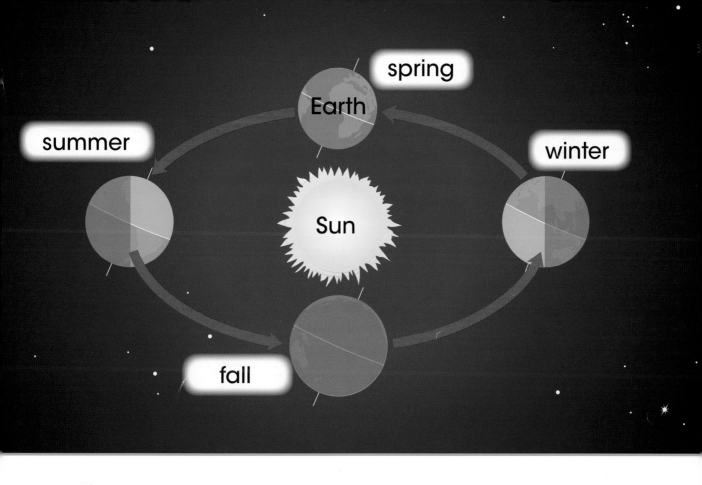

The seasons change as the Earth travels around the Sun.

Winter

In winter we feel the cold.

In winter we taste hot chocolate.

In winter we hear the wind.

In winter we see bare trees.

Spring

In spring we feel warm weather.

In spring we hear birds sing.

In spring we see new plants.

In spring we smell flowers.

Summer

In summer we feel the heat.

In summer we see the bright Sun.

In summer we taste fresh berries.

In summer we hear water splash.

Fall

In fall we feel cool air.

In fall we hear leaves crunch.

(16) In fall we feel a warm sweater.

In fall we see birds flying south.

In fall we see leaves change color.

Around the World

Some places are always cold.

Some places are always hot.

We use a calendar to know the season.

see hear feel taste smell

We use our senses to know the season.

What are the seasons like where you live?

Picture Glossary

Earth the planet on which we live

Sun the star that gives heat and light to the Earth; the Earth travels around the Sun

Index

Note to Parents and Teachers

Before reading

Discuss the current season and characteristics of that season where you live. Prompt children to think about the different clothing they might wear during different seasons. Review the five senses with children and begin a discussion of things that they see, hear, smell, feel, and taste each season.

After reading

- Collect photos that illustrate different seasons and use as a sorting activity.
- You might explain to children that a season also refers to a certain time of year that is characterized by a particular event or activity (e.g., strawberry season, football season, allergy season). Encourage them to name and identify other seasons with which they are familiar.